D0930284

Mary Lou,
    To my dear and
longtime friend.
        Enjoy,
            Judy

12/92

Harmony

Text copyright © MCMXCI Hazelden Foundation®
Art copyright © MCMXCI The C.R. Gibson Company
No portion of this publication may
be reproduced in any manner without
written permission of the publisher.
Published by The C.R. Gibson Company
Knight Street, Norwalk, Connecticut
Printed in the United States of America
All rights reserved.

ISBN 0-8378-2047-2
GB684

Harmony

·Hazelden Encouragements·

Illustrated by
Jody Bishel and Daniel Buckley

The C.R. Gibson Company
Norwalk, Connecticut 06856

Harmony

⁓

*Let me seek harmony,
through calmness, grace,
and contentment.*

*Let me claim as mine
the rocks, the color purple,
simple things, even pain.*

*Let me affirm myself
worthy of love, whole and
complete, yet not perfect.*

Let me be ever attentive
to my inner voice, my feelings
my dreams, my purpose.

Let me celebrate my power
by loving, forgiving, growing,
making a difference.

Let me be not an island
but related, connected,
woven into life's tapestry.

Let me seek a life in harmony
with myself and all things.

Stephanie Oda

Life Song

When a pianist learns a new piece of music, he or she often needs to practice each hand's work separately to learn the feel, to learn the sound. One hand picks out a part until there is a rhythm and ease in playing what is difficult. Then, the musician practices with the other hand, picking through the notes, one by one, until that hand learns its tasks. When each hand has learned its part—the sound, the feel, the rhythm, the tones—then both hands can play together.

During this time of practice, the music may sound disconnected, not particularly beautiful. But when both hands are ready to play together, music is created—a whole piece comes together in harmony and beauty.

When we begin to change our life for the better we may spend months, even years, practicing. We take our new skills into our work, our career, and begin to apply them slowly, making our work relationships healthier for us. We take our skills into our personal relationships...one relationship at a time. We struggle through our new behaviors in our love relationships.

One part at a time, we practice our new music note by note.

We work on our relationship with our Higher Power—our spirituality. We work at believing we deserve the best. We work on our finances... our recreation...on our appearance...on our home. We work on feelings...beliefs...behaviors.

Letting go of the old, acquiring the new. We work and work and work. We practice. It may all seem disconnected. It may not sound like a harmonious, beautiful piece of music—just isolated notes. Then one day, something happens. We become ready to play with both hands, to put the music together.

What we have been working toward, note by note, becomes a song. That song is a whole life, a complete life, a life in harmony.

Melody Beattie

Harmony is everywhere.
I will celebrate it.
I will trust the present.
I will trust the future.

Grace

I believe most people are aware of periods in their lives when they seem to be "in grace" and other periods when they feel "out of grace," even though they may use different words to describe these states. In the first happy condition, one seems to carry all one's tasks before one lightly, as if borne along on a great tide; and in the opposite state one can hardly tie a shoestring.

It is true that a large part of life consists in learning a technique of tying the shoestring, whether one is in grace or not. But there are techniques of living too; there are even techniques in the search for grace. And techniques can be cultivated.

Ann Morrow Lindbergh

Listen to the music of today.
Get in tune, in rhythm.
You are needed
for the concert's beauty.

Contentment

On the evening of the first day of spring, a woman gave her husband a bright red geranium in a clay pot. To celebrate, he placed it on the window sill, and together they marvelled at the delicate petals.

In the harsher light of morning, though, the man frowned at the geranium and said to his wife, "How shabby it makes the sofa look." They spent the day at the furniture store and came home with a new couch, blue with red flowers, like the geranium. They placed the couch in front of the window sill and together admired its grace and line and fashionable upholstery.

The next morning the man frowned at the couch and said, "How shabby it makes the carpet look." Soon they had a lavish new carpet, which led to new curtains, lamps, and chairs. When the room was completely redone, they set

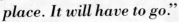the geranium back in the window and surveyed
the finest room in the neighborhood. The man
frowned. "The geranium," he said. "It's out of
place. It will have to go."

It is wealth to be content.

Lao-Tzu

*If one only wished to be happy,
this could be easily accomplished;
but we wish to be happier than other people,
and this is always difficult,
for we believe others
to be happier than they are.*

Charles de Secondat Montesquieu

Creation

*E*ach snowflake that falls from the sky has a different pattern. Every fall foliage season is a spectacular pallet of oranges, reds and yellows. The height of the giant redwoods is astounding, as is their ability to thrive with a road cut through their base. The rainbow after a rainstorm, the camouflage of nature's insects and animals, and the majesty of the mountains are just a few of the natural wonders of the world.

Today we can slow down the pace and notice the things around us. If we can quietly think about these things for a few minutes, we can begin to notice the creations of our Higher Power and appreciate their beauty.

❦

*Nature, the Gentlest Mother, is
Impatient of no Child...*

Emily Dickinson

*That I am here
is a wonderful mystery
to which joy is
the natural response.*

To live is to open ourselves to possibility, to rule out nothing. There is no way we can spare ourselves, or those we love, the pains of living, because they are inseparable from the joys. How grandiose we are when we think we can save the world.

All we can do—and it's quite a lot—is to live the best way we can, achieving a balance amid the forces that pull on us: pleasure, responsibility, power, love. If we can live so that we respond to all of them, rule out none, we will have the best the world can give.

Worthiness

The seeds that grow pear trees don't yield perfect trees. Some of the fruit is ripe and juicy; some hard and dry; some fruit never matures. Yet the pear tree will be a good tree if it's tended with care. So it is with us. Every part of us may not be perfect, but with care we can make the best person possible from the God seed that began us.

When we notice our own tree is not perfect, it becomes easier to forgive the blights of those around us. It is also important to forgive ourselves our faults. Though all the trees are beautiful, they each have their scars. Being human means we are, like all humanity, both beautiful and imperfect.

It is always a mistake
not to close one's eyes,
whether to forgive
or look better into oneself.

Maurice Maeterlinck

The need to know that we count in the lives of others, that our presence has not gone unnoticed, is universal. Few of us are blessed from birth with full knowledge of our connectedness to all life. Instead we falter and fumble our way through our experiences, uncertain of our worth and meaning. Acceptance by others is our want. Unconditional love is our due. Since we all share this same need to be acknowledged, it's best we each offer acknowledgement to those sharing our experiences today. They aren't unlike us; their needs and insecurities match our own. We'd all survive the harsh bumps of life with so much greater ease if we felt the comfort of others. In the company of others nothing is too much for any of us to handle.

Feelings

How do we become needed? We have only to look at our own needs and give what we need to others—love, respect, kindness, generosity. When we realize we are needed, we realize we also need others.

*My attitude
will make this day
what it becomes.
Meeting it head on,
with love, will assure
me of a lovely day.*

Each of us has a little voice inside, relentless as a chirping cricket, telling us what to do. Even in the middle of the toughest decisions, we always have within us a solution that is right for us. All we have to do is listen—and trust.

I'm grateful for my feelings; they're close to my capacity for love.

Love

Most of all,
let love guide your life...

Colossians 3:4

What in the world is love? It doesn't live in a tree or a book, so where in the world do we look? Can we find love in the house, maybe swept under a rug? Can we know the feel of it in our hands, see it written on the lines of the faces we know? Does it make a sound—maybe laugh or cry? Does it know how to speak, form words carefully, write letters? Is it only written on the heart?

We find it inside us, and our love seeks itself out in others. We find it in the familiar footfall of a brother and sister, the sound of a parent's voice in the next room. Too often we don't express love directly. When we do, our love thrives in all we do together.

*Look into the hearts
of people you encounter today
and offer them love.*

I like not only to be loved,
but also to be told that I am loved...
the realm of silence is large enough
beyond the grave.

George Eliot

The expression of love

softens us and the ones we love.

It opens a channel between us.

It invites an intimate response

that closes the distance.

Freedom to live, to grow, to experience my full capabilities is as close as my faith. I will cling only to that and discover the love that's truly in my heart and the hearts of my loved ones.

Mutuality

Safe in our own homes, or deep into our jobs, it's difficult to remember that we're part of the indivisible life of each, and that everything we do affects that "network of mutuality," just as we're affected by it.

Stop and think of the beautiful image of the arctic tundra, or the atmospheric envelope. These are parts of the world that we may have thought of as inert, nonliving, until we learned how delicate their sensitivity is to everything that touches them.

Everything touches them, as everything touches us. We are as much a part of the rhythm of life as the delicate web of roots that hold the permafrost in place. The same over-arching world spirit inhabits us, and we are as necessary as molecules of oxygen.

At last, we have achieved the capacity to communicate with our fellow human beings. Let us hope we can do it as well as sparrows do, or grass, for we can shape our destiny even as we're shaped by it.

*W*e are related to every person we see in a day, from the bus driver to the family member, from the store clerk to the boss, from strangers on the sidewalk to our dear friends. We are constantly changing, in constant motion with the people, places, and things around us. We are connected like links in a chain. Each link supports and gets support from those around it.

*S*ucceeding alone means we have survived; succeeding with others means we have truly lived. We are not put into this life to survive without others, but to live with them. By joining ourselves with the humanity around us, we have joined that spirit which connects us all.

My beauty today
will be enhanced
by my gentle attention
to the other people
sharing my experiences.

You cannot shake hands
with a clenched fist.

Indira Ghandi

Creation is interdependent. Every element, every human, every organism is necessary to the completion of the whole. How comforting to know that our existence is not mere chance. The space we take here, now, is advancing the development of all aspects of life. We never need to doubt our value, our importance to others. Being alive is the ultimate proof that each of us is necessary to the many persons in our lives. Gratitude for them and for us, will strengthen our understanding.

Life Song

So few people understand the benefits of celebrating life as it's received. Finding pleasure in the ordinary occurrences heightens our awareness that, indeed, no occurrence is truly ordinary. Every moment is special.

How wonderful that life always offers us
room to grow! It makes new discoveries possible
all through our lives, and ensures us that we will
always have something to offer.

*A*s an old man walked along the beach at dawn, he noticed a young man ahead of him picking up starfish and flinging them into the sea. Finally catching up with the youth, he asked him why he was doing this. The answer was that the stranded starfish would die if left until the morning sun.

"But the beach goes on for miles and there are millions of starfish," countered the other. "How can your effort make any difference?"

The young man looked at the starfish in his hand and then threw it to safety in the waves. "It makes a difference to this one," he said.

*For there is a music
wherever there is harmony,
order or proportion;
and thus far we may maintain
the music of the spheres;
for those well ordered motions,
and regular paces,
though they give no sound unto the ear,
yet to the understanding they strike
a note most full of harmony.*

Sir Thomas Browne

Colophon

Compiled and edited by Stephanie C. Oda
Designed by Aurora Campanella Lyman
Calligraphed by Martin Holloway
Type set in Kunstler Script, Bodoni Book Italic